WHO'S *that* DOGGY?

Mike Meehan and Alissa Murphy

Who's That Doggy?
Copyright © 2015
Story and Illustrations by Mike Meehan
First Edition - April 2015
whosthatdoggy.com
twitter.com/petfriendlystl

Photography by Mike Meehan, 1, 4, 5, 9, 12, 13, 20, 21, 24, 25, 28, 29, 30, 32, 40, 41, 44

Photography by Alissa Murphy, 8, 17, 33, 37

Photography by VIP Vacation Photography, Debra Collins, Dave Rivard, 16, 36

ISBN: 978-0692421253

A portion of the net proceeds from the sales of this book go to animal rescue and care programs.

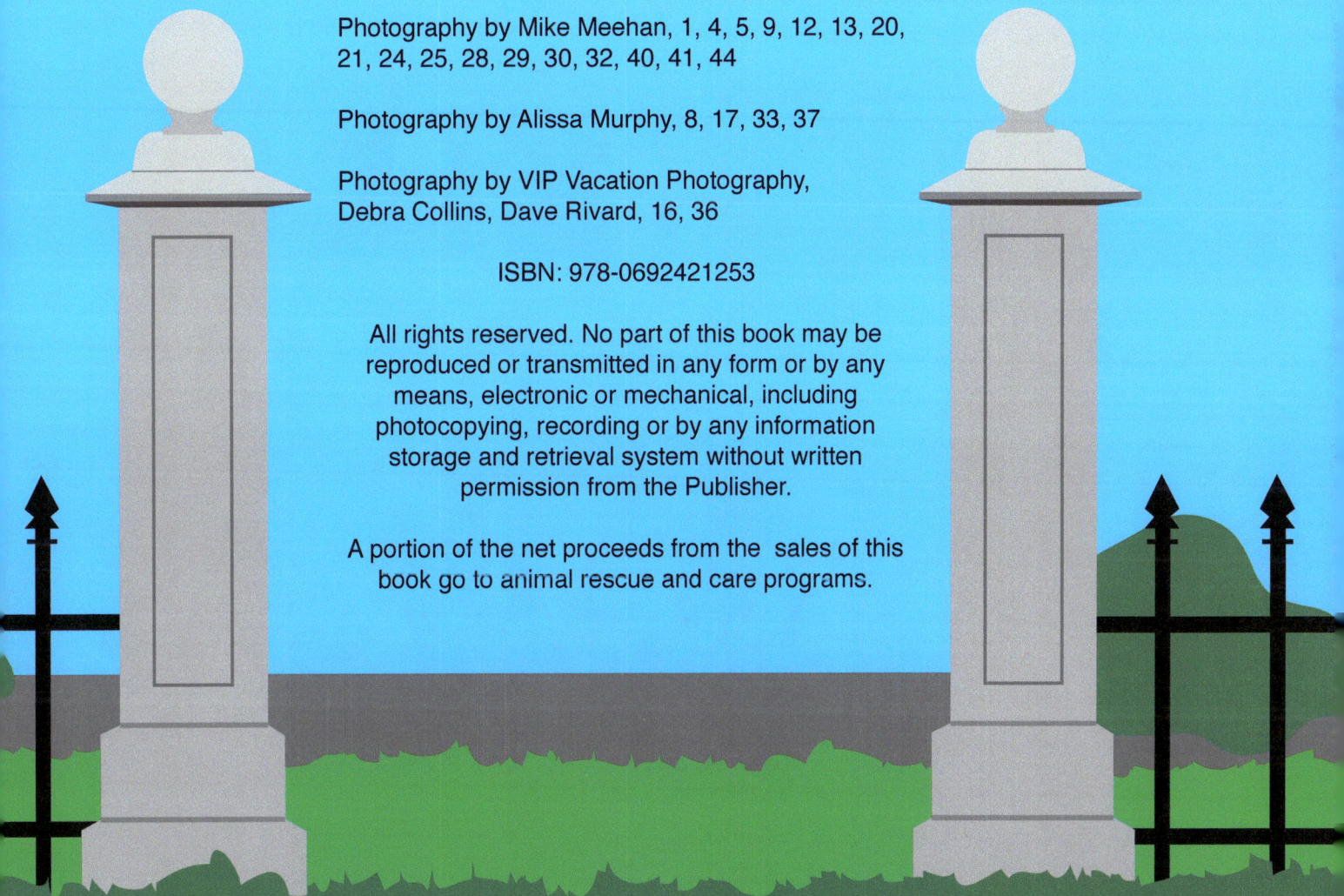

WHO'S *that* DOGGY?

Mike Meehan and Alissa Murphy

This is the story of Jon Jon, an American Cocker Spaniel who was brought to the Humane Society of Missouri as a stray in 2009.

The Humane Society staff treated and cared for Jon Jon for weeks before he was well enough for adoption. When he became healthy, he was quickly adopted by Alissa Murphy.

"Who's That Doggy?" tells his story, and many other dogs like him, who were lost or abandoned. Through the care of organizations like the Humane Society, Animal Protective Association and Stray Rescue, they begin wonderful lives with their new families.

A portion of the proceeds from the sales of this book go to animal rescue and care organizations to help other pets like Jon Jon.

ANIMAL RESCUE & ADOPTION
SUPPORTER

WHO'S *that* DOGGY?

Mike Meehan and Alissa Murphy

JON JON

I don't know how I ended up there,
I needed out of the pound.

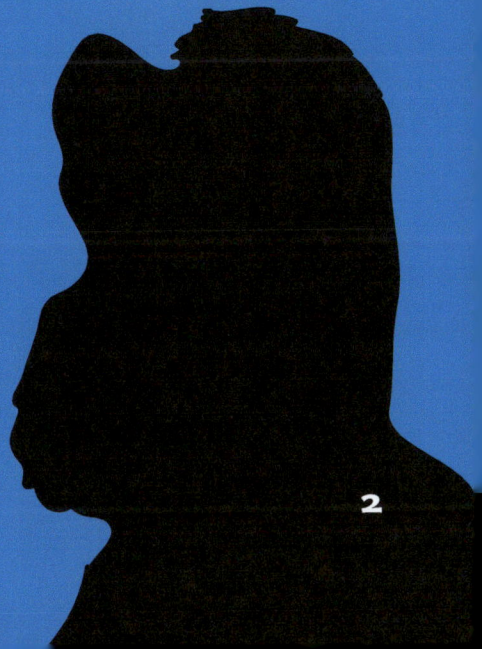

2

From the beginning you could tell,
I wasn't an ordinary hound.

3

Purina Beggin'® Pet Parade

4

APA Canine Carnival

5

I was tired of my cage
and really wanted a ma.

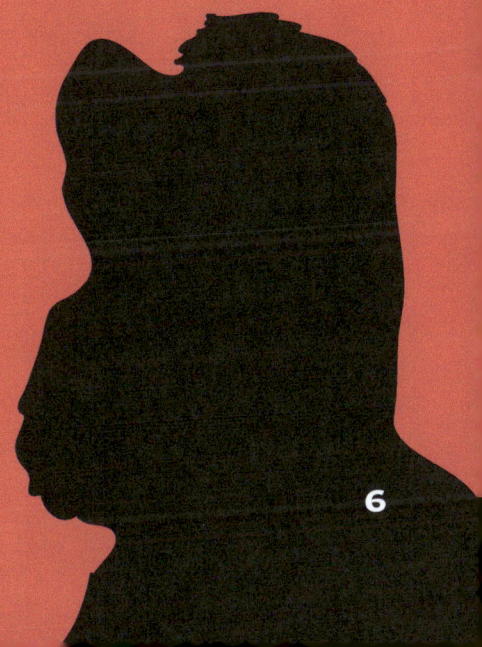

6

So when you stopped by,
I gave you my paw.

7

After weeks of waiting
you gave me a new home,

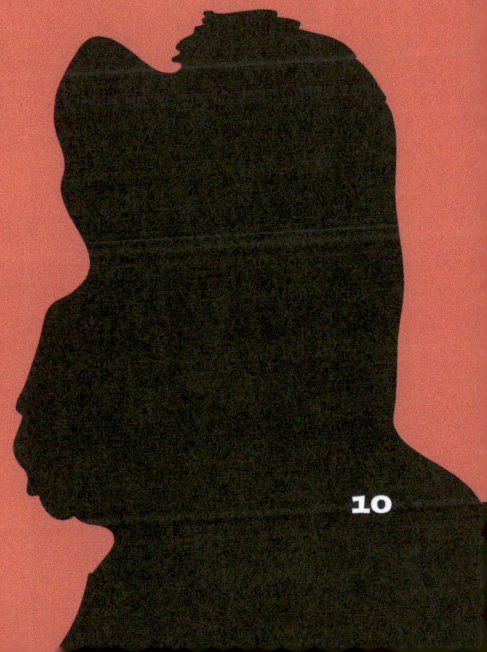

**with plenty of space
to play, jump and roam.**

11

Now instead of being lonely
and left all alone,

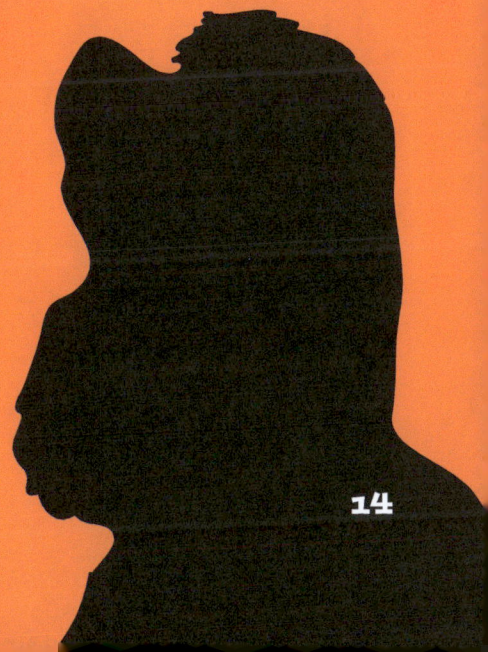

I now have a family
that I can call all my own.

Mr. Squirrel and Mr. Duck
are my favorite toys to maul,

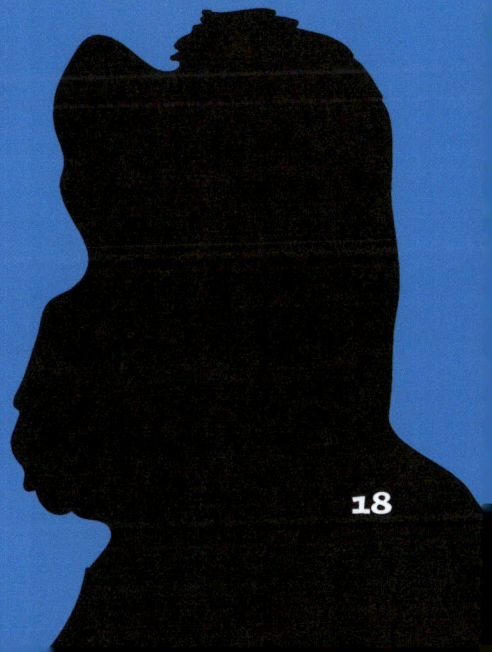

but what I love most is to play with my ball.

Squirrels and rabbits
I give good chase,

but catching those critters
is never the case.

Easter Egg Hunts at Treats Unleashed and Four Muddy Paws

There's never a shortage
of fun things to do.

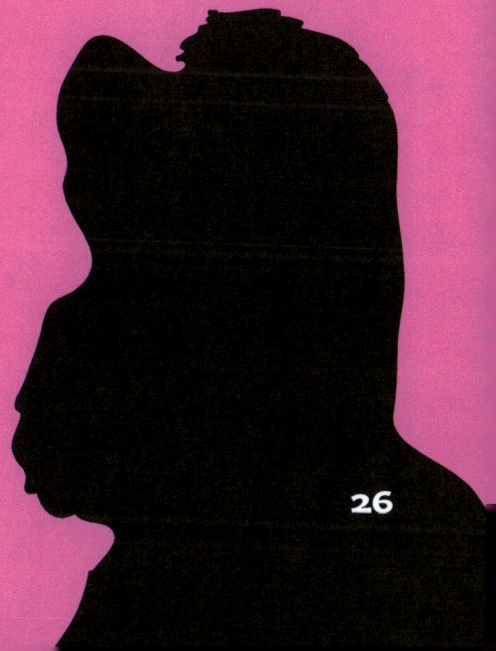

I've experienced so many
things that are new.

27

Sledding on Art Hill

The wind in my face
when I ride in the Jeep,

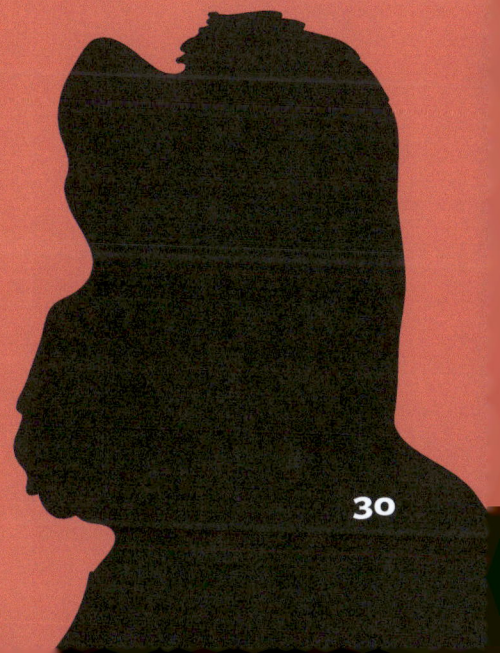

**buckled in safely,
so I don't take a leap.**

31

APA Fast & Furriest 5K

33

A romp in the park
or a game of fetch,

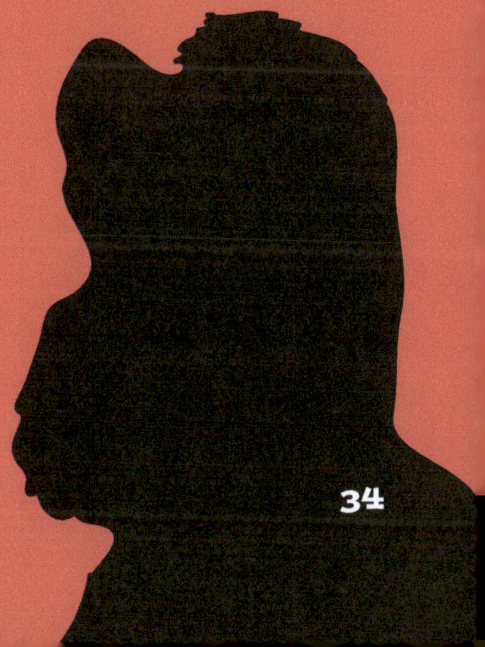

you knew from the beginning
I was a good catch.

Sometimes I'm known
as the black furry creature.

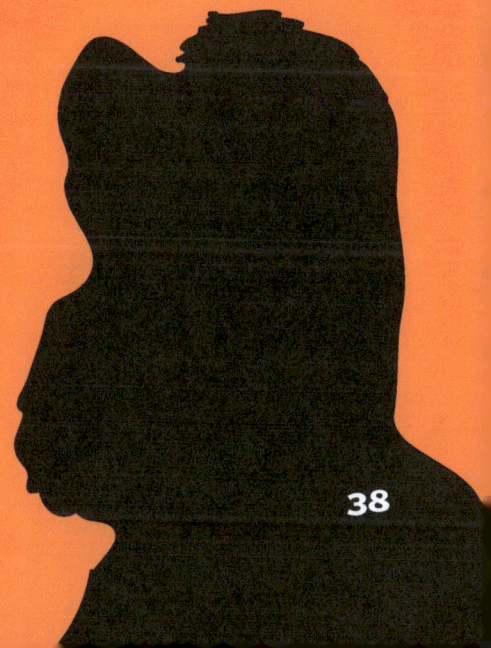

My shiny black coat is
my distinguishing feature.

Purina Pooches in the Ballpark

41

Since you adopted me
you've had no remorse.

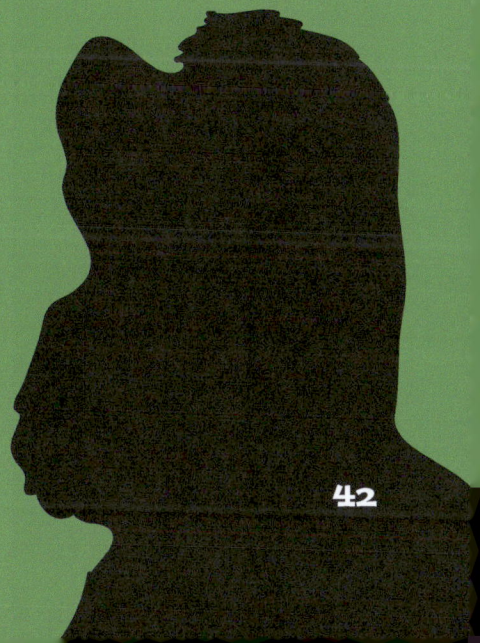

Who's that doggy?
It's Jon Jon of course!

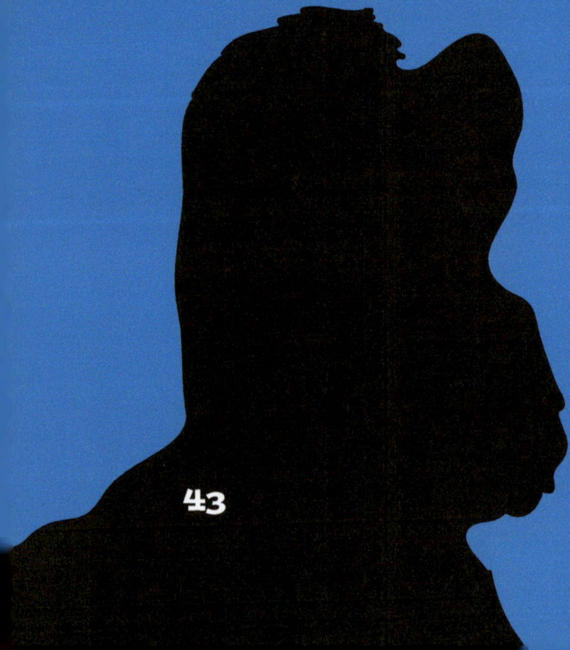

44

St. Louis is a great city for you to explore with your pet!

Events

Beggin' Pet Parade
February / March
beggin.com/pet-parade

APA Fast and Furriest 5K
April
apamo.org

St. Louis Earth Day
April
stlouisearthday.org

HSMO Bark in the Park
May
hsmo.org/bark

Urban Wanderers Exhibit Stray Rescue of St. Louis
June/July
strayrescue.org

Pooches In The Ballpark
July
cardinals.com

Paddle With Your Pooch
July
boathouseforestpark.com/

Community Swimming Pool Parties
September

Maplewood Family
Aquatic Center
mo-maplewood.civicplus.com

University City
Heman Park Pool
ucitymo.org

APA Canine Carnival
October
apamo.org/

CWE Halloween Pet Parade
October
thecwe.com/

Visit petfriendlystl.com for more information
on pet friendly places in St. Louis.

Here are a few of Jon Jon's favorite places and events.

Places

The Cheshire
cheshirestl.com

Chandler Hill Vineyards
chandlerhillvineyards.com

Four Muddy Paws
fourmuddypaws.com

Forest Park
forestparkforever.org

Lola and Penelopes
lolaandpenelopes.com

Lafayette Square Park
lafayettesquare.org

Museum of the Dog
museumofthedog.org

Purina Farms
purinafarms.com

Animal Rescue Organizations

Animal Protective Association
apamo.org

Humane Society of Missouri
hsmo.org

Stray Rescue of St. Louis
strayrescue.org

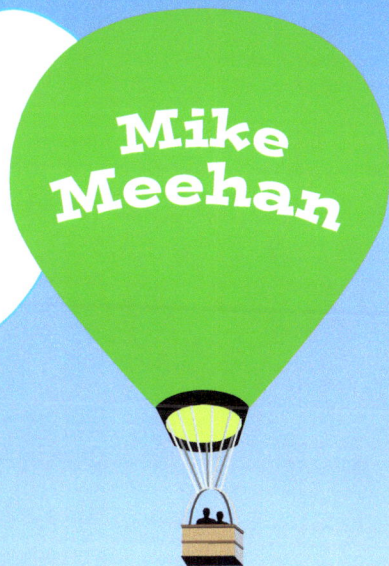

Mike Meehan grew up in St. Mary's-of-the-Woods, Indiana before moving to St. Louis in 2004. He is a writer and artist and a graduate of Indiana State University and Saint Louis University, He wrote, illustrated and provided much of the photography for this book.

Jon Jon is an American cocker spaniel who was adopted from the Humane Society of Missouri in November 2009. "Who's That Doggy?" tells the story of his adoption and the joy that he has brought to his new family.

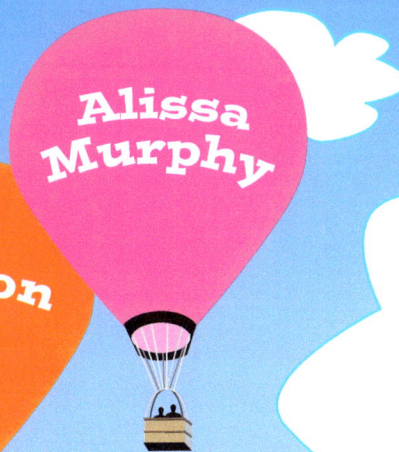

Alissa Murphy is a St. Louis native and a graduate of Saint Mary's College in Notre Dame, Indiana. In 2009, she adopted Jon Jon from the Humane Society of Missouri. Many of her photos are featured in this book. She has worked in healthcare sales for over 17 years.

www.ingramcontent.com/pod-product-compliance
Lightning Source LLC
LaVergne TN
LVHW072134070426
835513LV00003B/98